TABLE OF CONTENTS

A Pelican Book

Teaching Tips for Caregivers and Teachers:

Research shows that one of the best ways for students to learn a new topic is to read about it.

Before Reading

- Read the title and predict what the book will be about.
- Read the "Words to Know" and discuss the meaning of each word.
- Read the back cover to see what the book is about.

During Reading

- When a student gets to a word that is unknown, ask them to look at the rest of the sentence to find clues to help with the meaning of the unknown word.
- Motivate students with praise and encouragement.

After Reading

- Discuss the main idea of the book.
- Ask students to give one detail that they learned in the book.

Sight Words

a	get	ride
all	have	some
around	I	the
by	on	two

Words to Know

bike

handlebars

light

pedals

road

wheels

I get around by **bike**.

bike

All bikes have two **wheels**.

wheels

pedal

All bikes have **pedals**.

handlebar

All bikes have **handlebars.**

Some bikes have a **light**.

light

Some bikes ride on the **road**.

road

Index

Written by: Ryan Earley
Design by: Niko Magaro
Editor: Kim Thompson
Series Development: James Earley

Photos: All images from Shutterstock

Library of Congress PCN Data
Bikes / Ryan Earley
How I Get Around
ISBN 979-8-8945-9259-6(hard cover)
ISBN 979-8-8945-9273-2(paperback)
ISBN 979-8-8945-9301-2(EPUB)
ISBN 979-8-8945-9287-9(eBook)
ISBN 979-8-8945-9315-9(audio)
ISBN 979-8-8945-9329-6(Read-Along)
Library of Congress Control Number: 2024946362

Printed in Canada/012025/CP20250101

Seahorse Publishing Company
seahorsepub.com

Published in the United States
Seahorse Publishing
PO Box 771325
Coral Springs, FL 33077